FULL EMPLOYMENT IS A PRO-MARKET CONCEPT:
An Anthology

By: Jim Green

DEDICATED TO:

Making the world a better place….

ISBN-13: 978-1490577401

ISBN-10: 1490577408

CONTENTS

PROLOGUE

Most Americans are unaware that we have the legal authority—on the books, as I write—to end our unemployment crisis in America, tomorrow.

This bears repeating: *WE*, the American people, have the *LEGAL AUTHORITY* to end our unemployment crisis in America, on the books, thus raising the question: When we have 25 million unemployed/underemployed Americans, why on earth are our elected representatives in Washington not enforcing this "authorization"?

And the purpose of this book is to drill down on that question:

In his book, "The Audacity of Hope", President Obama stated that most Americans believe "that anybody willing to work should be able to find a job"—

Indeed, a Zogby poll found that 86% of Americans support this concept--so the solution to our unemployment crisis is not being undermined by a lack of political will on the part of the American people—

And the demand to fix unemployment existed *before* the Great Recession, with "Fix Unemployment" as a major battle cry in the 2008 election, *before* the economic meltdown—[which made it infinitely worse].

The data dates the problem to the early 1970's, and according to economic expert, Dr. William F. Mitchell, "High and persistent unemployment has pervaded almost every OECD country since the mid-1970's".

The OECD is a network of market-driven economies across the globe, formed in 1960, and includes the United States.

High unemployment is not limited to the OECD, however, and was also a major factor in Arab Spring.

And as a world leader, America should be leading the way in a fix, particularly since we have the legal authority to end this insidious "social" problem, tomorrow [see proposed solution, below]....

In the mid-1970's the world economy underwent a major paradigm shift, and while economists disagree over why, it is proposed, here, that the colliding forces of automation, technology, globalization, etc., reached a critical mass in the mid-1970's, resulting in ubiquitous unemployment in all of the OECD countries—

Eurozone unemployment is still in excess of 10%, with Greece and Spain far in excess of 20% youth unemployment, and America's numbers are all too familiar, above.

Further, since that time the market has been less and less able to create the jobs necessary to its viability [thus our pervasive unemployment], and while our leaders celebrated the benefits of automation to increase "profits" for the market, they have had "a deer in the headlights" regarding a solution for the displaced worker.

The operative words central to the thesis presented, here, are "market"—[saving it—I am a capitalist], and "unemployment" i.e., the market thrives when we have a robust, employed, consuming workforce....*and by failing to fix unemployment we both undermine the market, as well as exacerbate the "social" problems caused by unemployment!*

And a pervasive belief in the market-driven economies, is the myth that the "market" can create all the jobs we need—and coupled with the erroneous belief that jobs can *only* be created by the market.

This belief [sacred cow] has been a major stumbling block in our finding a solution to today's unemployment crisis—

And blindsides a *major factor* in unemployment—it is a "social" problem—We, the larger society, not the market, have the responsibility to fix—Indeed, fixing unemployment is antithetical to the objectives of the market [which is to make a profit, not solve social problems]--And we would not have a welfare system if the market was able to provide everyone with a job....

Indeed, every waking moment in a market economy is spent pondering how to eliminate as many of us humans, as possible, from the workplace—to increase "profits"—so why on earth would we hang our hat on the market solving our unemployment crisis? It doesn't make any sense...to reiterate, on our current path we both harm the market as well as exacerbate the "social" problems resulting from unemployment....it is a lose/lose proposition....

If someone "believes" they have the right solution, however, or believe a problem will be solved via "magical thinking" [virtually every Republican in Congress]—even when it is a myth, and results in a disaster---they are either unwilling, or unable, to consider alternative solutions....Building a ship to go around the world never even occurred to persons who believed the world was flat....and the same mind-set is at play here....

Also here, the world has changed, our solution to end unemployment hasn't, and in this case the myopia has been almost fatal [the jury is still out]—

Proof: the 2010 election, and currently a House full of the looniest, certifiable nut case extremists on the face of the earth [222 on the high end]—*in large part driven by racism*—and Hell-bent on creating an America unfit for human habitation, and in obstructing every viable solution proposed by President Obama solely for "political" reasons [and driven by their racist constituents]....

[Apologies for the colorful language, here, but it is honest, and a less strident description would not accurately describe this disaster for America]!

And as a consummate conservative insider in Washington observed regarding the Republican Party, today--"The Republicans went crazy"....[and as just one tiny example, as I write, Republicans in the Senate want to add $30 billion to our deficit—to appease their xenophobic constituents—building more fence and additional officers to prevent Mexicans from coming to America—when we have had 0 immigration from Mexico since 2007—we have as many going that way, as coming this way]—the insanity continues!

In short, when the Democrats failed to fix "unemployment"--the American people responded with a vengeance in the 2010 election [actually shot themselves in the foot—and rather than rioting in the streets as they are in Cairo, today 6/30/13, we rioted at the ballot box]—and resulting in America being hampered by this dumbing down of America, until at least 2020—our next census. More on this later....

We have two major paths to job creation in America, and to understand how we got here, we need to trace back over that history.

In an effort to provide employment for our returning troops, following WW II, President Truman signed into law THE FULL EMPLOYMENT ACT OF 1946.

This law was expanded upon in 1978, and as a direct response to the major economic shift in the mid-1970's, Congress passed, and President Carter signed into law: 15 USC § 3101--a Pro-Market solution—more on this later....

This law "*authorizes*" us, us Americans, to create a "reservoir of public employment" *anytime* our unemployment in America exceeds "3%" for persons over age 20, and "4%" for persons over age 16.

In short, at no time should our unemployment rate in America exceed 3%, for the vast majority of Americans....

But, save for a lone Congressman, Conyers of Michigan—enforcement of the above law to end our unemployment crisis, fell victim to our greed and ignorance, in America!

That is, Rep. Conyers' legislation, HR 870/4277, [and specific to the above "authorization"] died in Committee in the House on 1/3/13—along with the 112th Congress.

In summing up, on our current path the CBO projects that it will be 2017, before we can get back to even an anemic 5.5% unemployment rate—with unemployment benefits long since expired…but if the market fails in the interim, the unemployed are out of luck!

In short, Washington does not currently have any legislation *specific* to ending unemployment in America—[and in spite of the demands for same by the American people] but rather, is still operating on the mind-set:

Fix the market, which the Republicans ostensibly claim will create jobs [it is a lie—and which HR 2847—the Hire Act—proved *doesn't work!*]—when we should be doing the exact opposite, *fix unemployment, and this will fix the market* [the path we should be on]!

An important distinction needs to be made, here—The American Jobs Act—the well-intended legislation proposed by President

Obama—and for all the good intentions is still a "stop gap" solution—it does not address unemployment as a stand-alone "social" problem—in need of a permanent solution, and we as a society have the absolute responsibility to step in and solve, i.e., with *renewable funding*—rather than treading water until the Market can take over the problem...looking to the Market for the solution is absurd.....and also ignores the damage caused by unenmployment!

Fast forward to the importance of Social Insurance:

President Obama had a weapon in addressing our economic meltdown, not available to FDR during the Great Depression....Specifically, were it not for Social Security Insurance moneys percolating up through our economy in 2009—we would not be talking about having narrowly averted another Great Depression—*we would be buried in one!*

Social Insurance is the term used for our self-insurance, as a larger society—to address a ubiquitous social need—we don't want our streets lined with seniors or our disabled, with "Will Work For Food" signs [with the exception of Paul Ryan, and like black-hearted

Republicans]—and like all insurance we pool our money to protect us in case fate taps us on the shoulder.

And Social Insurance has the added benefit of creating stability in our market economy—and in moderating the adverse effects of the business cycle.

Incidentally, if you have picked up a bit of outrage regarding the Republican Party, today—we are on the same page--the Republican agenda has been a *major* stumbling block in ending our unemployment crisis in America, and it is an outrage *every* American should feel!

There are no moderate Republicans any more….it has been taken over by their extremists, and racists—and the national Republican Party has but a single agenda: To pander to the GREED of their wealthiest contributors—and they have a Treasonist indifference to the betterment of America!

Ironically, and running in parallel with the major economic shift, above, Republican Propaganda Mills started cropping up since the

1970's [and jokingly referred to as "think tanks"]—but with a single agenda:

To plot how to lie to the American people in the form of specious and blatantly false propaganda ads/wedge issues—to conceal their true agenda—defined above—and a spin-off is corrupt legislation via ALEC....[the goal of ALEC was to take over where Donald Sagretti left off—and is one of the most destructive forces in America, today—it poses far more of a threat to America, than terrorism]!

And part and parcel to this deception, "Tax Watchdogs" started cropping up all over the place—some by persons who would starve to death if others didn't pay theirs....[the rank and file Tea Party faction, etc.]....

The conservative "think tanks" do not ask the question "How can we build a strong and decent America?" --but rather asks "How can we steal everything that isn't nailed down in America?".... The question every American should be asking----[as a democracy, and in search of a decent America] "What kind of America do we want?" –is not even on the table....

This is relevant to our discussion, here, because it is essential in understanding the cultural contamination of the devious Republican agenda in undermining a fix to our unemployment crisis, in America—and the Republican agenda, today, is devoid of *any* socially redeeming value!

And as just one illustration, Social Security Insurance—is a Social Insurance, and most comparable to our auto insurance—we support everyone being covered because we don't want our fellow motorists to be uninsured—but have you ever heard of our auto insurance being referred to as an "entitlement"?

The knee-jerk reaction is to say, "Of course not, we pay for it, it is not a government giveaway program"—and that is the specific reason why the Republicans introduced this devious, destructive propaganda, and false term into our dialogue—[so their wealthiest contributors could avoid paying taxes—and based solely on their GREED!]—

And far from being a "government giveaway program", or being insolvent—Social Security Insurance, has historically brought in more than it pays out [does not add a dime to our deficit]—is solvent to 2037, and like *all* insurance, is subject to actuarial adjustments from time to time [the scare tactics are BS]!

There is only one reason Ryan's budget [and his ilk] want to destroy Social Security: PURE GREED—and his budget is based on the same old Supply-Side scam perpetrated on the American people, by the Republicans for the past 30 years!

The over-arching point, here, is that we can enforce the above "authorization" and end our unemployment crisis with *Social Insurance*, and without adding a dime to our deficit. Stay tuned.

Unfortunately, the image created by the detractors to "public employment" is that it would be a massive government program, adding billions of dollars to our deficit, with the federal government hiring millions of people— none of which is true, or necessary, to end our unemployment crisis—and being anti-Full Employment, undermines our market economies—not the other way around.....

Two Pro-Market, deficit-neutral solutions to Full Employment are posted here—if the reader can improve on either, by all means speak up....

Congressman Conyers' legislation, HR 870, is deficit-neutral, and would be funded with a very modest .25% tax on stock transactions. A trust account would be created by the Labor Department—and used to fund work/training projects proposed across the labor market, with emphasis on pockets of high unemployment—such as Indian reservations.

Similar in construct, but with a difference in funding, is as well deficit-neutral, Pro-Market: THE NEIGHBOR TO NEIGHBOR JOB CREATION ACT: A federally mandated Social Insurance, owned by our employed to provide a fund to hire/train our unemployed. For a modest 4% of salary policy cost we can reduce our unemployment to 3% within a year of passage. Further, this would create more "private sector" jobs in 6 months, than the path we are on now in 6 years!

Further, Jobs Beget Jobs....and by the year 2015 over 50% of the world's population will live in mega-cities, with many millions in population--and a truism going forward in the 21st Century, for our market economies, is that a "reservoir of pubic employment" is an *indispensable* component to the *effective functioning* of a modern market economy—and not the least in the interest of civil order! Our choices are change or build more and more prisons, etc......

The market is no longer capable of creating the jobs necessary to its viability—which will become progressively more true as we move forward in the 21st Century—[and the proliferation of more automation] --and it would appear to be a no-brainer that we have a sluggish recovery, because almost 14% [the true rate] are unemployed/underemployed!

Which raises the question: Why is Congress not working on deficit-neutral solutions, such as proposed here, given the "authorization" to reduce our unemployment to 3%--and so that we can end our unemployment crisis? The answer, I would suggest, is because "conventional wisdom" is still clinging to the "belief" to the last burning ember--that the market can solve/fix our unemployment crisis....[and in spite of overwhelming evidence to the contrary—and the damage caused in the interim]....

In creating a public workforce, however, every proposed solution should include the following:

1] It must be based on the premise that we have far more work that needs to be done in America—than we have persons to fill these jobs—[the notion that we would need "make work" jobs—is both a myth, and patently absurd]!

2] It must have renewable funding. This is *NOT* a "jump start" solution [such as HR 2847—HIRE Act]—i.e., funded until, in theory, the market will kick in and provide all the jobs we need [a fairy tale, at best, in any event]—

3] It will not add a dime to our deficit! Our unemployment is not the result of a lack of jobs, or money—but rather a lack of imagination—

4] It is based on the premise: Fix unemployment, and this will in turn fix the market—rather than the other way around—

5] Ideally, our Full Employment solution would be within THE BUFFER STOCK EMPLOYMENT MODEL: An expanding and contracting public workforce, that expands during downturns in the market [unemployment exceeds 3% in America], and contracts as employees return to the private sector [Google: Dr. William F. Mitchell, Australia].

If you paid attention during the Prologue you will not need to read the rest of the book [just kidding folks]....Indeed, the title says it all—the path we are on now harms the market, the American people, and America—and the mind-set, and path we should be on to fix this is:

FULL EMPLOYMENT IS A PRO-MARKET CONCEPT

Finally, the following letters expand on the above—and as Oscar Wilde averred "The only truly worthless opinion is an unbiased one"—so bias, agreed—but always in the interest in getting at the larger goal—the truth....

A note to the reader—the letters are mostly Letters to the Editor, or President Obama/Council of Economic Advisers--relative at the time--not in sequence, and some redundancy [please look for the nuggets...thx...lol...]—also, if you are a "typo-wonk"—are more concerned with sentence structure, etc., than content—you probably won't like my writing—and you will see a wayward capital letter, here and there, and appearing out of place and used for emphasis—editorial license—so apologies, here—

Just look for content, please....THX

CHAPTER ONE

President Obama/Council of Economic Advisers:

Capitalism is ideal in producing and selling corn flakes and cars—It doesn't work in solving "social problems" such as unemployment and our healthcare....

And when we have tried "privatization" to solve our social problems—it has been a disaster:

Essential programs have been cut—such as the elimination of text books from the Job Corps education program—to increase profits, and cronyism has been rampant—

And in our "for profit" healthcare system, billions of dollars are siphoned away from the premiums we send in—and do not go to the healthcare of ANYONE—but rather is used to pay for lobbyists, to make the CEO's filthy rich—and spent on propaganda ads to keep it that way!

Further, it attracts a few who see healthcare as a means to get rich, rather than cure the ill....

The truth is, we currently have a blended system—and they are, in fact, indispensable to each other:

Were it not for Social Security Insurance moneys percolating up through our economy in 2008—we would not be talking about having narrowly averted another Great Depression—We would be buried in one!

Social Insurance is a vital ingredient in building a vibrant and decent society—And, invent a better widget, sell the company for a million bucks, and retire in South Florida [capitalism]—is as well a vital ingredient in building a vibrant and decent society.

So why do we have this war of words pitting the two against each other—rather than educating the American people regarding the indispensable symbiotic relationship they have to each other?

Most Republicans ask God in their prayers at night to be protected from becoming communists, or socialists, or even worse "liberals"—

And this war of words disguises that the Republican Party, today, is not the Pro-Market party they boast—but rather their policies are, in fact, Anti-Market—destructive to capitalism!

Pandering to the GREED of their wealthiest contributors—the Republican One and Only program—is NOT a Pro-Market concept!

Another misnomer in the war of words, is right-wing invented "entitlement"—a word that should be banned from honest discussion—do we refer to our auto insurance as an "entitlement"?

And when Social Security Insurance brings in more that it pays out, i.e., is deficit-neutral--how is that an "entitlement", and why is it portrayed in our graphs as a "government expense"—or even included in these graphs? If a corporation reported a massive loss on a product they in fact made money—they would be charged with fraud in a New York Minute!

The list goes on—please see: OUR GREED AND IGNORANCE, on Amazon/Kindle

Jim Green, Democrat congressional opponent to Lamar Smith, 2000

CHAPTER TWO

THE HISTORY OF HOW WE GOT WHERE WE ARE:

In the mid-1970's, the colliding forces of automation, technology, globalization, etc., reached a critical mass—resulting in a Market no longer capable of producing the jobs necessary to its viability, and causing ubiquitous unemployment in all of the OECD countries-- leaving their leaders conflicted, ever since, regarding the displaced employee. Eurozone unemployment is still in double digits, and Greece and Spain both in excess of 20%, plus. High unemployment was also a major factor in Arab Spring.

In the U.S., we took a pro-active role in addressing this economic shift—and in 1978 President Carter signed into law 15 USC § 3101- -which "authorizes" the creation of a "reservoir of public employment" at any time our unemployment in America exceeds "3%".

In 1979, however, and in a panic over Humphrey-Hawkins—our ultra-conservative foundations, and desperate to promote the

Supply-Side fraud, embraced a flawed paper by an obscure MIT student, David L. Birch "The Job Generation Process"; and [with lots of cash] gave his paper biblical importance, and every president since has cited his finding as gospel.

Birch's paper concluded that "small businesses" were the greatest generator of new jobs— problem is, for the purposes of policy-making— it is BS. In a study at Harvard University in 2010, "The Myth of Small Business Job Creation" The research shows "no systematic relationship between firm size and growth." And that small businesses can actually detract from job growth.

In spite of this, however, Washington struggles, still, to make this antiquated notion, work--that it is only the market that can create jobs—and the result has been a disaster, politically as well as otherwise!

It would be impossible to still have 7.8% unemployment—if we were on the right path— and among other problems with this concept--if the market fails, the unemployed are out of luck.

Further, unemployment is a "social" problem we are seeking to address with a highly unstable, incompatible entity: The Market

What apparently isn't clear going forward is that an expanding and contracting public workforce is an INDISPENSABLE component to the correct functioning of a modern market economy—

The market thrives when we have a robust, employed, consuming workforce—and overlooked is that HR 870 [currently in Committee], and the proposed "Neighbor-To-Neighbor Job Creation Act" www.Inclusivism.org [both authorized under Humphrey-Hawkins], are deficit-neutral--Pro-Market "win-win" solutions:

The American people win, and capitalism wins—

Jim Green, Democrat candidate for Congress, 2000

CHAPTER THREE

Editor, NY TIMES:

America's public safety is at risk for a single reason—the Republicans in Congress! So when are we going to get honest about their devious agenda, and the hoodlums carrying it out?

Americans are currently being forced to endure the legacy of the most dangerous, and yes, most evil experiment in our history—"Neoliberalism" [Laissez-faire on steroids]:

The massive deregulation of the market—the siphoning of America's wealth away from the consuming middle, and transferring this wealth to the already most wealthy—via obscene tax cuts--AKA Supply-Side, AKA Reaganomics, ad nauseam!

It is evil, because it is based on lies—cotton candy—the deception was the promise of great rewards to the American people—our corporations would build factories all across America, with the windfall of cash—and via the Market jobs would trickle down like moonbeams—and everyone would have a job in the corporation—Yes, folks, it's a fairy tale!

Well, in fact, the most wealthy built factories, alright—in Indonesia—taking jobs away from Americans, and then hid their massive profits in the Cayman Islands—to evade paying taxes—in short, they have NO interest in the betterment of America—their agenda is about PURE GREED!

But even putting the GREED aspect aside, this scheme has a shelf life of about 7 years before it sends the economy into meltdown, as occurred in 1987 and in 2008—costing the taxpayers trillions to put a floor under a vanishing economy.

We cannot siphon America's wealth away from the consuming middle—without this result!

Further, the shortfall in revenue lost from the obscene tax cuts to the 1%, was added to our deficit—driving America into almost fatal debt!

Our deficit was a highly manageable $60 billion in 1980—when this fraud—the "Grand Experiment" was first perpetrated on the American people—by 2008 our debt had been run up to a staggering $10 trillion—and it has cost the American taxpayers an additional $6 trillion to clean up the mess caused by the Grand Experiment—and prevent another Great Depression!

And even more devious in carrying out this evil scheme--the Republicans distracted via our ignorant and uninformed with propaganda nonsense about contraception, and gay marriage, and their agenda to abolish women's civil rights—to cover-up their evil agenda, above! And has subjected America to the will of the ignorant and uninformed!

And this has given us jerks like Ted Cruz, and Paul Ryan, persons devoid of any common decency—and a Republican Party immersed in the "Grand Experiment"—to this day--in short, an agenda devoid of any socially redeeming value!

See: OUR GREED AND IGNORANCE, on Amazon/Kindle

Jim Green, Congressional Democrat opponent to Lamar Smith, 2000

CHAPTER FOUR

I would like to take credit for this—but I can't—I found it posted on a blog—and would give credit if the author would come forward—it is what President Roosevelt meant by "All we have to fear, is fear itself", and it is gripping America, today, and sapping away our energy—and is the source of our entropy—and if we fail, this will be the reason….

"Conservatives are such cowards: they are afraid of gay people getting married or serving in the military; they are afraid of bringing terrorists to super max prisons in the US from which no one has ever escaped; they are afraid of the boy scouts letting gay kids in; they are afraid of everyone voting and are constantly suppressing the vote under some bogus voter fraud theory; they are afraid of letting students vote at their universities; they are afraid of women having the right to choose; they even are afraid of women getting contraception [the real issue actually is a women's agency and control over their bodies]; they are afraid of immigration reform leading to citizenship because they are afraid of-- name whatever reason; they are afraid of mandating gun purchasers to undergo background checks for crazy people and terrorists; they are afraid of people smoking pot; they are afraid of climate change being real and contradicting their beloved Bible; they are afraid of legitimate campaign reform; they are afraid of Muslims; they are afraid of blacks; they are afraid of atheists; they are afraid of hippies; they are afraid of socialists; they are probably still afraid of monsters under their beds; they are just rank cowards and keep making things up to be afraid of....."

Anonymous

CHAPTER FIVE

ENDING OUR UNEMPLOYMENT CRISIS WILL BE AT RISK UNTIL WE FIX OUR ELECTRONIC VOTING NIGHTMARE [And particularly with the Court striking down a critical part of the Voting Rights Act, on 6/25/13]:

So long as the potential for manipulation of electronic voting continues to exist—our elections in America will be in peril! In spite of all the polls showing a strong Obama victory--it was not until 10PM Central on 11-4-08.....that we could breath a sigh of relief....we had been cheated out of the past two elections....with many believing that Bush was never legally elected president of the United States....and we were braced for the worst.......this can, and MUST be fixed before 2014, so that this never happens again, and in the interest of all who support fair and open elections--regardless of party. Accordingly, it is urged that we adopt the following proposed "FAIL-SAFE ELECTRONIC VOTING ACT":

THE FAIL-SAFE ELECTRONIC VOTING ACT

1) EVERY electronic voting machine (hereafter EVM), must be inexpensive, identical throughout the U.S. in a 1/150 ratio, and _must count and produce a hard-copy of the recorded votes_. In addition, an extra copy of their recorded votes would be produced (not necessarily a hard-copy), marked "Voter's Copy", and containing "NOTICE: Do Not Destroy Until Every Election On Your Ballot Is Certified". [If Wal-Mart handed us a paper with "trust us" as a receipt for our purchases—_We would be outraged!_ And yet that is our current electronic voting system—and this regards our democracy!].

2) _After confirming that their votes are recorded correctly_, the voter would then insert the hard-copy ballot into a software-free (count only) optical scanner (hereafter OS), for a second count. The hard-copy ballot would be retained by election officials in the event a candidate asks for a recount (_not possible under the current system, and which undermines the legality of each such election_). The EVM and the OS must be manufactured by different companies (which is universally true today).

3) Election officials assigned to oversee the EVM, would be prevented by law from

overseeing the OS, and vice-versa, and stiff criminal penalties would be imposed for violations.

4) Further, every EVM would be programmed with raw data re the total registration rolls, by party, and norms for their voting history, etc.,----as an "alert" to a possible irregularity, such as an "Under-vote"—or "vote-flipping" etc., and _standards_ established to suspend certification where there is an "improbable result", at least temporarily, of a particular election until the discrepancy is cleared up. (This is what computers do best, and it would be very easy to create such a program).

5) At the end of the election day, tallies would be taken from the EVM and the OS, for each candidate. _If the tallies didn't balance for any given election, or if there is an "alert", that election cannot be certified until the "error" is corrected._ If the candidates agree (the victory is certain), minor discrepancies in the count could be disregarded. While probably rare, the Voter, or a random sample of Voters, would be required by law to return their Copy of the recorded votes to the election office to clear up any "error", or where an "alert" signals the need for same.

6) Further, every state provides for a recount when the total vote falls below a certain percent of difference between the candidates, impossible to conduct with the current EVM—and thus Congress must mandate the following regarding presidential candidates: A RUN-OFF election is mandated and triggered in those states where the percent of total vote is less than .5% of difference between any given candidates; said election to be held on the second Saturday following the election, on PAPER BALLOTS ONLY, and contain ONLY the names of the relevant candidates, for instance: "Barack Obama, Democrat" and "John McCain, Republican"—with oversight in counting by a representative(s) of each party—said procedure providing more than adequate time to meet the Electoral College mandate. NOTE: Had this been the law in 2000, Al Gore would be our president, and the American economy would not be in meltdown!

7) Finally, absent the above safeguards, and until these safeguards are in place--Congress must mandate that PAPER BALLOTS, ONLY, can be used in our presidential elections. This is not a "partisan" issue, it is a "pro-democracy" issue. Most importantly, this will return the

responsibility for our elections, and our vote counting, back into the hands of the individual voter, where it belongs, and out of the hands of "corporate control"---*it is after all "our democracy", itself, that is at risk if we don't take these steps---and in that regard, is there any time or cost differential that is too great?*

Reply To: Jim Green -- Democrat candidate for Congress, Dist 21, TX, 2000

CHAPTER SIX

President Obama/Council of Economic Advisers:

PRISON REFORM:

The world economy underwent a paradigm shift in the mid-1970's, resulting from the colliding forces of automation, technology, globalization, etc., reaching a critical mass---And since the mid-1970's the Market has been unable to create the jobs necessary to its viability—With the result that "High and persistent unemployment has pervaded almost every OECD country since the mid-1970's." [Dr. William F. Mitchell].

Our choices in the U.S. were: Adapt and change our laws so that we could apply solutions that would effectively address this cosmic shift in the economy---Or, create a prison system [turn America into a Police State] so that we could hold in place our antiquated solutions....

We chose the latter, and by 1990 we had passed up every other country on earth in locking people up—and currently we have 5% of the world's population, and 25% [one in four] of all prison inmates on Earth, in our prisons! We have the same number incarcerated as China, but they have a billion more people!

Further, by applying antiquated solutions during the Great Rescission, and rather than change—we currently have 25 million unemployed/under-employed Americans—and the CBO projecting it will be 2017 before we get back to even an anemic 5.5% jobless rate—and unemployment benefits long since expired!

The truth is, the world has changed, our solution to end unemployment hasn't, and the result has been a disaster [the 2010 election….].

Ironically, in 1978, the U.S. responded directly to the above economic shift in the mid-1970's, and President Carter signed into law 15 USC § 3101, which "authorizes" the creation of a "reservoir of public employees", anytime our jobless rate exceeded "3%"—a Pro-Market solution--the law was misunderstood, however, and to this day has never been implemented [and in spite of HR 870].

Missing in our current solution, and mind-set: Full Employment is indispensable in creating a decent society, while Unemployment harms the individual, the market, and the larger society!

And accordingly, the path we should be on, and proposed, here, is a Pro-Market, deficit-neutral The Neighbor-To-Neighbor Job Creation Act: A federally mandated Social Insurance—owned by our employed to provide a fund to hire/train our unemployed. For a modest 4% of salary policy cost we can reduce our unemployment to 3% within a year of passage.

See also: ECONOMIC INCLUSIVISM, on Amazon/Kindle

Jim Green, Democrat opponent to Lamar Smith for Congress, 2000

CHAPTER SEVEN

President Obama/Economic Advisers:

Unemployment is a "social" problem, we as a society, must solve—fix--

In "The Audacity of Hope" President Obama reported a pervasive mind-set on the part of the American people: "Most of them thought that anybody willing to work should be able to find a job....". A recent Zogby poll found that "86% of Americans" agree—

And as a democracy—it is not the American people standing in the way of this being a reality—the following is a framework for making it the law of the land:

If one is working--then they must chip in to help their neighbor get a job--and the vast majority of Americans ask: Why have you waited so long to ask us, Washington?

In creating "The Neighbor-To-Neighbor Job Creation Act" [hereafter NTN] it must contain the following:

1] It must be based on the premise that we have far more work that needs to be done in America—than we have persons to fill these jobs—[the notion that we would need "make work" jobs—is both a myth, and patently absurd]!

2] It must have renewable funding. This is NOT a "jump start" solution [such as HR 2847—HIRE Act]—i.e., funded until, in theory, the market will provide all the jobs we need [a fairy tale, at best, in any event]—

3] It will not add a dime to our deficit! Our unemployment is not the result of a lack of jobs, or money—but rather a lack of imagination—NTN is outlined, below.

4] It is based on the premise: Fix unemployment, and this will in turn fix the market—rather than the other way around—which is the flaw in our "conventional wisdom" today—and the reason why we still have 25 million unemployed, or underemployed, and a sluggish recovery. Also, disregarded is that if the market fails, the unemployed are out of luck!

5] NTN is a federally mandated, mutual insurance—owned by our employed to provide a fund to hire/train our unemployed. And the infrastructure is already in place via FICA.

6] Using The Buffer Stock Employment Model—[an expanding and contracting public workforce—and an INDISPENSABLE component in a modern market economy]— NTN would be triggered anytime our unemployment exceeds 3%--and contract as employees return to the private sector.

7] For a modest policy cost of 4% of salary we can reduce our unemployment, within a year of passage, to 3%—and as "authorized" in Public Law 15 USC § 3101. For comprehensive detail see: www.Inclusivism.org –HR 870 [currently in Committee], and "OUR GREED AND IGNORANCE, on Amazon/Kindle

Jim Green, Democrat candidate for Congress, 2000

CHAPTER EIGHT

President Obama:

Over the past 65 years two American presidents have signed into law—what every politician since the beginning of our republic have promised—but have never delivered: Full Employment.

Finally, our politicians had specific "authorization" to end unemployment in America, permanently—and not the least of importance in these laws—of indispensable importance to capitalism—the market thrives when we have a robust, employed, consuming workforce.

The Full Employment Act of 1946 [Truman]; and the Humphrey-Hawkins Full Employment Act [1978 – Carter--hereafter H-H] –But in spite of the fact that both of these are laws on our books in the United States – neither have ever been implemented –

And also in spite of the fact that they are supported by some of our most eminent economists—John Kenneth Galbraith for one,

and of vital importance to the American economy, and the American people!

Blindsided by myths and sacred cows—we still have one foot on the plantation—virtually all of our laws see American employees as a "pool of slaves" to be used and discarded "at will"—and our politicians still quake from the ghost of McCarthyism [not that it has any relevance, whatsoever].

In 1998, an eminent Australian economist, Dr. William Mitchell, presented a paper at the University of Chicago, which framed up the model all of our market economies have no choice but to adopt in the future, and totally consistent with H-H: The Buffer Stock Employment Model [hereafter, BSE].

The fact is, we have become victims of our success—and around 1975 the colliding forces of globalization/automation/technology reached a critical mass—resulting in ubiquitous unemployment affecting all of the the OECD countries—including the U.S, and has ever since left our leaders befuddled re: what to do with the displaced employee?

The BSE model provides an answer, and not the least to preserve capitalism: A permanent expanding and contracting public workforce—that expands during downturns in the market, and contracts as employees return to the private sector.

We have millions of infrastructure jobs, in every jurisdiction in America, that every year go unfilled—and 14 millions unemployed—and yet, so far, we have been unable to use one to fix the other—and fix both in the process!

And we can fund without adding a dime to our deficit with a federally mandated, mutual insurance—owned by the American employee to hire/train our unemployed:
www.Inclusivism.org

Jim Green, Democrat candidate for Congress, 2000

CHAPTER NINE

The following is my original web page, which has been on the internet since 1996—www.Inclusivism.org---it has undergone a few incarnations—but from the beginning has observed the following: The world has changed, our solutions haven't, and too often the result has been a disaster [the 2010 election]—but given this observation it was queried:

Given that the world has changed what should we be doing so that we can accurately adapt/adjust to our 21st Century world? The following are the proposed steps [bifurcated solutions] we need to take so that we are in concert with the world we live in....[concerned, yes, arrogant, no—and hopefully seen as the result of critical thinking] and denial that the world has changed is not an option—the world is going to change whether we like it or not.....

ECONOMIC INCLUSIVISM: Neo-Capitalism--Inclusive pro-market solutions to our social problems

"There is one thing stronger than all the armies in the world: and that is an idea whose time has come." Victor Hugo

[Social/Prison Reforms]

1) We need to re-classify all crime in the future as "violent" or "non-violent", and discard the archaic terms "felony" and "misdemeanor". The word felony has been implanted in the public's mind to mean "armed and dangerous"....and yet over 70% of our prison inmates (all felons)are in prison for non-violent offenses....as a result, the term "felony" is distracting us from addressing the real problem....the violent offender.

2) We need a much greater use of "Shock" Incarceration (A sentencing alternative I authored in the 1960's); a greater use of fines and probation (both civil and criminal), in lieu of incarceration, and an expanded menu of sentencing alternatives. We have 5% of the world's population, and 25% of all prison inmates on earth, in our prisons! We have the same number incarcerated as China, but they have a billion more people! If we had the same proportion of inmates to general population as the rest of the civilized world, we would have

400,000 persons incarcerated, not over 2,200,000, as we do at present! And yet our PR is that we are the most free country in the world? We daily turn non-violent persons into violent career criminals, with over 99% released back into society, making life in America MORE dangerous, not less! Prison should be a last resort, not first.

3) We need the creation of Federal Regional Diagnostic and Treatment Centers, for the diagnosis and treatment of the violent offender. We have learned a great deal about violent behavior in recent years (see www.brainplace.com), and yet we do not have a cohesive or concerted national program or policy in America for dealing with this national epidemic and disgrace. The sheer numbers of homicides by handguns, alone, tells the whole story: Canada 151, Australia 57, Germany 373, Japan 19, England and Wales 54, the United States 11,789 [numbers which remain static, year after year]! And, when we add in all deaths by guns, including the fact that 9 children are killed by guns everyday in America, our gun violence escalates to a staggering 28,663! Also, we need to allow for voluntary admissions to these Centers, to prevent juvenile and family violence. It is essential that we seek out

"problem-solving", not "punishment" oriented solutions, which actually exacerbate crime. [As a brief addendum, here—this was originally written 15 years ago—not as the horrible disaster at Sandy Hook]--

4) We need to pick-up the lead taken by England, in treating drug addiction as a "medical" rather than a "criminal" problem, so that we can EFFECTIVELY curb drug-related crime, and keep drugs out of the hands of our youth. To demonstrate how specious our thinking has become in this area, alcohol and tobacco kill ten of thousands of persons annually, and yet these drugs are not classified as "dangerous". The tiny handful of persons with "addictive personalities" has totally shaped our drug policies while "addiction", in all of its forms, can only EFFECTIVELY be treated with a medical solution. We have wasted billions on interdiction, and yet, youth drug abuse is actually increasing.

[Economic Reforms]

5) To address our insidious practice of "exclusion", Congress must enforce a citizen's legal right to work, as enacted by Congress in "The Full Employment Act of 1946", and

reaffirmed in 1978--and as outlined in the Democratic National Platform position asserting "Opportunity to every American". The right to work and be a productive member of one's society is also a human right. Accordingly, we must ratify the following constitutional amendment: "Work shall hereafter be the legal right of every citizen, and Congress shall, except for retirement/disability programs under federal jurisdiction, make no laws which will abridge the right of any citizen of legal age, to work and be a productive citizen." [Our lapse in enlightenment regarding this urgently needed systemic change -- believed by the ignorant and uninformed to be "socialism or communism" – and combined with some really peculiar notions about guns, is the cause for almost all violent crime in America]. Outlined in more detail, herein--

6) To ensure enforcement/fund this legal right, Congress would create a privately owned, federally mandated, Social Insurance plan, owned by our employed to provide a fund to hire/train our unemployed. Work could include: Child care for low income working families, building a high-speed rail system, the urgent need outlined by the NEA for School Modernization, the creation of Federal Regional

Diagnostic and Treatment Centers for the diagnosis and treatment of the violent offender, repairing our rotting infrastructure [the list of social benefits is endless]. As owners of this plan, each worker could vote on proposed national projects and dividends would be paid annually from unused funds. A projected policy cost of 4% of salary would reduce our unemployment to 3%, within a year of passage, and as "authorized" under Public Law . [Like Social Security and military retirement moneys, Economic Inclusivism would _strengthen_, not weaken the business community....these steps are necessary to preserve, not harm capitalism in a rapidly changing economy....and prevent our further movement down the erroneous path towards communism or towards the other extreme, fascism (our current movement), both of which require a dictator, and the wholesale loss of our civil liberties, to hold the government in place.]

7) Since this program of "inclusion" would address 95% of our social ills (crime, welfare, drugs, etc., and exacerbated in many cases by inept Band-Aid programs), the federal budget could be greatly reduced and our current Federal Income Tax would be replaced with a National Sales Tax, value-added tax, a national

lottery, or some combination of taxes other than our current Federal Income Tax. We currently spend $14 billion annually for the Internal Revenue Service, and corporations and individuals spend trillions trying to get around the Tax Code, all of which is passed on to us, the consumer, in the higher cost of consumer goods.

CHAPTER TEN

April 18, 2013

PART 1 [of 2] April Jobs Report

F. Michael Kelleher, Special Assistant to President Obama

President Obama/Council of Economic Advisers:

Since the mid-1970's, the Market has been less, and less, capable of creating the jobs necessary to its viability—and going forward in the 21st Century, an expanding and contracting public workforce is an—*indispensable*--component to the effective functioning of a modern market economy.

Every credible economist agrees with Dr. William F. Mitchell that "High and persistent unemployment has pervaded almost every OECD country since the mid-1970's.".

In the mid-1970's, the world economy underwent a paradigm shift: The colliding forces of automation, technology, globalization, etc., reached a critical mass—resulting in ubiquitous unemployment in all of the OECD countries— leaving their leaders conflicted, ever since, regarding the displaced employee.

Eurozone unemployment is still in double digits, with Greece and Spain both in excess of 20%, and we still have 12 million jobless Americans, in spite of our optimistic, but lethargic, 7.6% unemployment rate.

In the U.S., we took a pro-active role in addressing this economic shift—and in 1978 President Carter signed into law 15 USC § 3101--which "authorizes" the creation of a "reservoir of public employment" anytime unemployment in America exceeds "3%"--a Pro-Market solution.

In Australia, Dr. Mitchell has proposed THE BUFFER STOCK EMPLOYMENT MODEL: An expanding and contracting public workforce, that expands during downturns in the market, and contracts as employees return to the private sector, and in applying our Law--triggered anytime our unemployment rate exceeds 3%.

PART 2 [of 2] April Jobs Report

For multiple reasons, the legacy of fear associated with McCarthyism, the erroneous belief that public sector jobs equate with massive deficit spending [given our $16 trillion debt], laboring under antiquated, and currently destructive, economic theory [Friedman] that only the market can create jobs, and the overarching reason: The failure to recognize unemployment as a "social" problem, i.e., we, as a society, are compelled to address—But as a result, Washington keeps insisting that the market can fix a problem—it is no longer capable of fixing--i.e., pervasive unemployment--and apparently oblivious to a truism under this scenario: If the market fails, the unemployed are out of luck--

In short, the world has changed, our solution hasn't, and fixing unemployment has been a disaster [the 2010 election: The public supports "anybody willing to work should be able to get a job" and when we failed to fix unemployment, the electorate responded with a vengeance.....for example, we celebrate automation, but are remiss in addressing the displaced employee].

And not being considered are Pro-Market, deficit-neutral solutions: HR 870 [funded by a stock transaction fee], and The Neighbor-To-

Neighbor Job Creation Act: A federally mandated, mutual insurance, owned by our employed—to provide a fund to hire/train our unemployed [via Social Insurance]. For a modest 4% of salary policy cost, we could reduce our unemployment to 3%, within a year of passage [and in concert with 86% of Americans who believe that "anybody willing to work should be able to find a job"].

In closing, jobs beget jobs--and this would create more private sector jobs in 6 months, than our current path [HR 2847—The HIRE Act], in six years....and evidenced by the CBO projection that on our current path it will take until 2017 just to get back to an anemic 5.5% unemployment rate [with unemployment benefits long since expired]—and for not the least of reasons, this would restore and inspire confidence in the economy, and address domestic violence—[and the failure by the Senate to pass common sense gun control was one of he most shameful days in American history!].

See also: ECONOMIC INCLUSIVISM, and BACK TO FULL EMPLOYMENT, on Amazon/Kindle.

Jim Green, Congressional Democrat opponent to Lamar Smith, 2000

CHAPTER ELEVEN

AUSTRALIA'S FULL EMPLOYMENT ACT:

President Obama/Fellow Democrats:

For the past 65 years we have had two parallel paths to address unemployment in America—

To assure employment for the troops returning from WW II, President Truman signed into law The Full Employment Act of 1946—

This was expanded upon in 1978 with the Humphrey-Hawkins Full Employment Act, signed into law by President Carter—

And a 21st Century version of this path to full employment in America, is pending the House, HR 870.

Humphrey-Hawkins best defines this path to addressing unemployment in America, and it "authorizes" our government to create a "reservoir of public employees" anytime our unemployment rises above "3%".

And in spite of the fact that this path to employment has been the law of the land since

1946—and is a Pro-Market solution [more on this shortly]---Washington has lacked the wherewithal to implement this path to employment on behalf of the American people—[a point not lost on the "occupy" movement].

Rather, Washington has taken the alternate parallel path—by insisting that human labor is a "component" in the free enterprise system—[barely distinguishable from the machine the human operates] to be used and discarded "at will"—and the Republican propaganda is that it is an attack upon "freedom" to challenge this concept, but whose "freedom"?

As a result, however, "conventional wisdom" has insisted that it is the market, alone, that can fix our unemployment crisis—the result has been a disaster—

The market thrives when we have a robust, employed, consuming public—and by taking this parallel path—we not only have a staggering 8.1% unemployment, but a struggling recovery as well.

Ironically, following WW II, Australia passed a law very similar to our Full Employment Act of 1946—

Difference is—they actually put it into effect—
and over the next 30 years—[until the cold
winds of conservatism swept in Reagan and
Thatcher, etc.] –the government in Australia
saw as a solemn responsibility that "anyone
willing to work should be provided with a job"
[a quote from the "Audacity of Hope"].

The citizens of Australia still refer to this 30
years as their "Golden Age".

Jim Green, Democrat candidate for Congress,
2000 www.Inclusivism.org

CHAPTER TWELVE

PRESIDENT OBAMA GOT BAD ADVICE....

President Obama/Fellow Democrats:

On June 13, 2011—Larry Summers, President Obama's first, and former, Director of the National Economic Council, projected that our unemployment rate should be down to 8% before the 2012 election—

Based on this projection we can definitively say that as an advisor on "unemployment"—[and in particular during the Great Recession]—President Obama could have gotten worse advice from his top economic advisor—but it is difficult to see how—

Professor Summers was brilliant in understanding the fix re our investment banking, but horrible in his understanding the cause and results of unemployment--And we have 24 million Americans unemployed or underemployed as proof!

There is no rational explanation why our unemployment rate in America, today, should exceed 3%—None—

Had Director Summers [our "conventional wisdom"] actually understood this social/economic/political problem and how to solve it—

We would have had legislation in the hopper and/or enforced existing legislation [15 USC § 3101]-- within the first 90 days, and we Americans would have been well on our way to 3% unemployment by the end of 2009—

Further, had this been the case, the American people, currently, would be considering an amendment to our Constitution so that President Obama could serve more than two terms—rather than seriously considering limiting to one—

To illustrate, we would never condemn the CEO for closing a plant, if they are losing money— but the American people are outraged by a government that lacks the imagination and wherewithal to step up to the plate with a solution to this lapse in our market system—

And at present we are asking the market to fix itself with both hands tied behind its back—by inexplicably, looking upon government involvement as if it were the plague, and insisting upon solving our unemployment crisis with "private sector jobs"—a concept that is antithetical to capitalism!

Full Employment is a Pro-Market concept—the market thrives when we have a robust, employed, consuming public – and we have far more jobs that need to be done in America, in every jurisdiction in America, than we have persons to fill these jobs—

While America drowns in myths and sacred cows-

The bottom line is, HR 870 [currently in Committee] can fix our unemployment crisis without adding a dime to our deficit, see also: www.Inclusivism.org –and are "win-win" solutions—the American people win, and capitalism wins!

Jim Green, Democrat candidate for Congress, 2000

CHAPTER THIRTEEN

Editor, NY TIMES:

SUPPLY-SIDE HAS A SHELF LIFE OF SEVEN YEARS OF WASTE AND FRAUD BEFORE IT SENDS OUR ECONOMY INTO MELTDOWN....

When are we going to get honest about the Republican agenda in America?

Americans are currently being forced to endure the legacy of the most dangerous, and yes, most evil experiment in our history—"Neoliberalism" [Laissez-faire on steroids]:

The massive deregulation of the market—the siphoning of America's wealth away from the consuming middle, and transferring this wealth to the already most wealthy—via obscene tax cuts--AKA Supply-Side, AKA Reaganomics, ad nauseam!

It is evil, because it is based on lies—cotton candy—it promised great rewards to the American people—our corporations would build factories all across America, with the windfall of cash—and via the Market jobs would trickle down like moonbeams—and everyone would have a job in the corporation—Yes, folks, it's a fairy tale!

Well, in fact, the most wealthy built factories, alright—in Indonesia—taking jobs away from Americans, and then hid their massive profits in the Cayman Islands—to evade paying taxes—in short, they have NO interest in the betterment of America—their agenda is about PURE GREED!

But even putting the GREED aspect aside, this scheme has a shelf life of about 7 years before it sends the economy into meltdown, as occurred in 1987 and in 2008.

We cannot siphon America's wealth away from the consuming middle—without this result! Further, the shortfall in revenue lost from the obscene tax cuts to the 1%, was added to our deficit—driving America into almost fatal debt!

Our deficit was a highly manageable $60 billion in 1980—when this fraud—the "Grand Experiment" was first perpetrated on the American people—by 2008 our debt had been run up to a staggering $10 trillion—and it has cost the American taxpayers an additional $6 trillion to clean up the mess caused by the

Grand Experiment—and prevent another Great Depression!

And even more devious in carrying out this evil scheme--the Republicans distracted via our ignorant and uninformed with nonsense about contraception, and gay marriage, and their agenda to abolish women's civil rights—to cover-up their evil agenda, above! And has subjected America to the will of the ignorant and uninformed!

And this has given us jerks like Ted Cruz, and Paul Ryan, persons devoid of any common decency—and a Republican Party immersed in the "Grand Experiment"—to this day--in short, an agenda devoid of any socially redeeming value!

See: OUR GREED AND IGNORANCE, on Amazon/Kindle

Jim Green, Congressional Democrat opponent to Lamar Smith, 2000

CHAPTER FOURTEEN

President Obama/Fellow Democrats--

There is a famous line from F. Scott Fitzgerald's "The Great Gatsby" regarding the carelessness of Tom and Daisy---a wealthy couple—and I'll paraphrase--they "smash up things and then retreat back into their money, leaving it to others to clean up their mess"

Is this not the quintessential definition of the Republican Party over the past 30 years?

U.S. Representative Ron Paul, a doctrinaire Libertarian—in an interview on CNN 4-21-11--was more pointed when he asserted that we played right into bin Laden's hand—squandering our wealth in America on Iraq and Afghanistan, etc.—and bringing our economy to the brink of collapse—which Paul asserts finished bin Laden's attack on 9-11-

And whether bin Laden could actually read us that well--—Congressman Paul was dead-on correct with the end result—

Further, our economic collapse in 1987 should have served as fair warning that Supply-Side

Economics has a shelf-life of only about 7 years before the economy starts caving in on itself—

We can't siphon America's wealth away from the consuming middle—the 98% of us [by giving obscene tax cuts for the top 2%] without sending our economy into a tailspin!

But by not learning from this lesson, we had to relive it again in 2008—only this time it created the worst economic disaster since the Great Depression!

And in the greatest shift upward of wealth in our history under S-SE—400 persons now hold more of American's wealth than 150 million of the rest of us do!

Further, we need to remind the Republicans in the Senate and House who espouse, daily, that cutting taxes for the 2% will solve our unemployment crisis [the Republican's one and only job creation solution]—That this is what we are doing NOW—[the tax cuts were extended] and it has left us with 14 million Americans still unemployed!

And finally, how anyone could buy into Congressman Paul Ryan's deficit reduction plan—Supply-Side Economics on steroids—is beyond human comprehension! Republican Conservative, and 30-year Congressional insider, Mike Lofgren, nailed it in his book title, regarding the Republican Party, today--with the "Republicans went crazy"....

Jim Green, Democrat candidate for Congress, 2000

CHAPTER FIFTEEN

F. Michael Kelleher

President Obama/Council of Economic Advisers:

RE: UNEMPLOYMENT IN TURKEY.....

The most perplexing question facing Americans today is: Why is our unemployment rate not 3%, or lower, in America?

We have the "legal authority" to reduce our unemployment rate to 3% [15 USC § 3101]—

And, we have the "political authority" to end our unemployment crisis—Most Americans believe that "anybody willing to work should be able to find a job...."

It is not the American people standing in the way of a solution—and FULL EMPLOYMENT IS A PRO-MARKET CONCEPT...[Source: Common Sense].

So why, at present, do we not have a single bill pending or proposed in Washington that is SPECIFICALLY directed to end unemployment? [HR 870 died in Committee, along with the 112th Congress]

In 2013, Believing the market can create all the jobs we need, ranks alongside believing the world was flat 1013—it is both erroneous, and a myth—[and yet, a belief held by a virtually every Republican in Congress, and far too many Democrats in Washington]....

A myth that prevents us from applying solutions that will actually end our unemployment crisis, and in the face of glaring empirical evidence that it is an erroneous belief....

That is, the mere existence of "Welfare", is the proof that "anybody willing to work should be able to find a job" does not exist in America, and in spite of this being the will of the majority of Americans!

Singularly, "Unemployment" is by far and away the most important, and pervasive, social problem facing America today:

Full Employment is an indispensable component in creating a decent society, while Unemployment causes incalculable damage to the individual, the market, and to the larger society—

It is obvious that myths and sacred cows have created antiquated and unworkable solutions— solutions that no longer work in a modern market economy [that has changed while our solutions haven't] --that has created the Gordian Knot, standing in the way of solving this pervasive social problem.

Advocated, here, is Pro-Market, deficit-neutral "The Neighbor-To-Neighbor Job Creation Act": A federally mandated Social Insurance, owned by our employed, to provide a fund to hire/train our unemployed. For a modest 4% of salary policy cost we can reduce our unemployment to 3% within a year of passage.

For a more in-depth look at the impact of this myth on the larger society, please see: THE HARVARD BOYS CLUB, on Amazon/Kindle

Jim Green, Democrat opponent to Lamar Smith for Congress, 2000

CHAPTER SIXTEEN

President Obama/Council of Economic Advisers:

A truism cited by Dr. William F. Mitchell "The Great Depression taught us that without government intervention, capitalism is inherently unstable and prone to delivering lengthy periods of unemployment."

Further, the jobs created by capitalism are for the express purpose of "increasing profits"—expecting this methodology to address the "social" problem of unemployment—is patently insane—and antithetical to the objectives of capitalism—and yet, this is precisely the path Washington—[locked into antiquated Friedman economic theory]--is following….

And, most alarming—is the absence of alarm over the CBO projection that on our current path it will be 2017 before we return to even an anemic 5.5% unemployment—[with unemployment benefits long since expired]—and the belief in Washington that this is somehow OK?

Where is the hue and cry in Washington that this is not acceptable, not now, not ever!

How did our "brightest and best" got duped into thinking this is OK?

Where is the exploration into alternative paths to end our unemployment crisis? 86% of Americans believe that "anybody willing to work should be able to find a job"—but Washington isn't listening....

The world has changed, our methodology hasn't, and the result has been a disaster [the 2010 election...]

Since the mid-1970's, the Market has been less, and less, capable of creating the jobs necessary to its viability—and going forward in the 21st Century, an expanding and contracting public workforce is an—*indispensable*--component to the effective functioning of a modern market economy.

In the mid-1970's, the world economy underwent a paradigm shift: The colliding forces of automation, technology, globalization, etc., reached a critical mass—resulting in ubiquitous unemployment in all of the OECD countries—leaving their leaders conflicted, ever since, regarding the displaced employee. [We celebrate automation and then get a "deer in the headlights" look re the displaced employee].

In the U.S., we took a pro-active role in addressing this economic shift—and in 1978 President Carter signed into law 15 USC § 3101--which "authorizes" the creation of a "reservoir of public employment" anytime unemployment in America exceeds "3%"--a Pro-Market solution.

So why are HR 870/The Neighbor-To-Neighbor Job Creation Act [deficit-neutral solutions] being ignored?

See also: ECONOMIC INCLUSIVISM on Amazon/Kindle.

Jim Green, Congressional Democrat opponent to Lamar Smith, 2000

CHAPTER SEVENTEEN

Saved the best for last....

This book is how "belief systems" have prevented us from solving our unemployment crisis—has undermined our market economy [I am a capitalist], and has left us with 25 million unemployed/underemployed Americans—but the belief
where we went off the rails—for instance, caused one zany Republican congressman to claim that males masturbate in the womb--is the "belief" that "sex is a sin"—and we took a very "natural and healthy" part of our life, and made it "dirty and nasty"—the following sums up this dilemma.....

[I couldn't resist including this...and yes I am the author.....]

A MESSAGE FROM GOD

MANY CENTURIES AGO, a man of the cloth, we don't know his name, and in a flash of insight (perhaps induced by peyote) told his flock that "sex is a sin". And lo and behold he learned that by taking a very natural and healthy part of our life and turning it into something that was "dirty and nasty", that he could imprison his flock, and fill his coffers, and hallelujah it was a great day for the Lord!

Quickly, his miracle spread to other churches in his village, and then to the next village, and then the next county, and then state, and soon it spread to all the churches in the ancient world, and all of their flocks cowed in fear and shame and became imprisoned, and their coffers over-floweth. Hallelujah, it was a great day for the Lord!

And to keep the myth alive they started inventing stories, half-baked stories, that made no sense to anyone who is rational, such as "Mary was a virgin"—well, she just had to be a virgin because she would never partake in anything that was dirty and nasty, like sex (if you're doing it right), and this was necessary to make "sex is a sin" make sense...so they invented a Mary that was "sinless"--you get the picture. And their coffers over-floweth. Hallelujah, it was a great day for the Lord!

No one seemed to be bothered that when we play tricks on the human mind by taking something that is very natural and healthy, such as sex, and make it dirty and nasty that all kinds of bad things happen to the human mind:

Such as most pedophiles, and most serial killers, and voting Republican, and unwarranted suicides, and most mental illness, and unwanted pregnancies. (Teens not wanting to have sex is the perversion, not the other way around, and by replacing sex education and condoms, with unrealistic "abstinence", and by using blather about "low self-esteem" to shame them into not "sinning"—We have a teen pregnancy in the U.S. twice that of England and Canada!).

But none of this mattered, because their coffers over-floweth, and Hallelujah, it is a great day for the Lord!

There is a cure--------Tell these right-wing loonies to shove it....

GOD

ABOUT THE AUTHOR: I was employed in our Criminal Justice System for a cumulative 20 years as a probation officer, with 5 of those years as a chief probation officer. I authored the concept of "Shock Incarceration" which became law in Kansas in 1970, and then was adopted in numerous jurisdictions in the U.S. and also spread to Europe—it is currently identified in the U.S. as "Boot Camp" [as the means to "shock" the young offender—and a total distortion of my original intent—like many ideas, once released, they take on a life of their own]. I also instigated establishment of the first Court Psychiatric Clinic in the U.S., in conjunction with psychiatrists from the Menninger Foundation, as a chief probation officer. Finally, I was the Democrat candidate for Congress, District 21, TX, 2000. I would most define myself as a Social Ecologist-- [albeit my

degree is in Psychology]. My web page is
www.Inclusivism.org –which has been on the
internet since 1996.

OTHER BOOKS BY THIS AUTHOR ON AMAZON/KINDLE/BN:

- THE HARVARD BOYS CLUB: Hitler's Assault On Our Freedoms From His Grave
- MY LETTERS TO PRESIDENT OBAMA: Confessions Of A Compulsive Letter Writer
- OUR GREED AND IGNORANCE: Poses A Far Greater Danger To America, Than Terrorism
- LETTERS ON STEROIDS: Confessions Of A Compulsive Letter-To-The-Editor Writer
- THE FIRST TIME I HAD SEX: And, The Religious Intolerance Attack On America
- WHY PRESIDENT OBAMA LOST THE 2012 ELECTION: A Wake-Up Call
- ECONOMIC INCLUSIVISM: Neo-Capitalism/An Anthology—Inclusive pro-market solutions to our social problems
- AMERICA IS ONE SICK MF: Why Greed-Driven America Went Off The Rails....
- EVERY GIVEN SUNDAY: A Scientific Formula To Predict NFL games

- **IT IS IMPOSSIBLE TO BE A CHRISTIAN, AND VOTE REPUBLICAN: An Anthology**
- **A POOL OF SLAVES: To Be Used And Discarded "at will"**

"Excellent , excellent . A fine blend of truths, half-truth, and blatant falsehoods."

IN THE

Supreme Court of the United States

October Term, 1979

No. 79-1627

JAMES L. GREEN,

Petitioner,

vs.

www.ingramcontent.com/pod-product-compliance
Lightning Source LLC
Chambersburg PA
CBHW051346170526
45166CB00002B/977